BEASTS AND THE BATTLE

BEASTLY ARMOUR

MILITARY DEFENCES INSPIRED BY ANIMALS

Charles C. Hofer

raintree
a Capstone company — publishers for children

Raintree is an imprint of Capstone Global Library Limited, a company incorporated in England and Wales having its registered office at 264 Banbury Road, Oxford, OX2 7DY – Registered company number: 6695582

www.raintree.co.uk
myorders@raintree.co.uk

Text © Capstone Global Library Limited 2021
The moral rights of the proprietor have been asserted.

All rights reserved. No part of this publication may be reproduced in any form or by any means (including photocopying or storing it in any medium by electronic means and whether or not transiently or incidentally to some other use of this publication) without the written permission of the copyright owner, except in accordance with the provisions of the Copyright, Designs and Patents Act 1988 or under the terms of a licence issued by the Copyright Licensing Agency, Barnard's Inn, 86 Fetter Lane, London, EC4A 1EN (www.cla.co.uk). Applications for the copyright owner's written permission should be addressed to the publisher.

Edited by Aaron Sautter
Designed by Kyle Grenz
Original illustrations © Capstone Global Library Limited 2021
Picture research by Morgan Walters
Production by Katy LaVigne
Originated by Capstone Global Library Ltd

978 1 4747 9385 8 (hardback)
978 1 4747 9393 3 (paperback)

British Library Cataloguing in Publication Data
A full catalogue record for this book is available from the British Library.

Acknowledgements
We would like to thank the following for permission to reproduce photographs:
Flickr: U.S. Army photo by Tom Faulkner, bottom left 20; Getty Images: IWM/Getty Images, 17, U.S. Navy, 19; Newscom: Album / Metropolitan Museum of Art, NY, bottom right 9, De Agostini / G. Dagli Orti Universal Images Group, (statue) 13; Shutterstock: AlejandroCarnicero, 25, alessandro guerriero, (man) 11, Alexander Tolstykh, 23, Anton Kozyrev, (beetle) 28, arka38, 4, Avatar_023, (vest) Cover, Borhax, (map) 5, BPTU, 26, Cristina Romero Palma, bottom right 20, Dan Thornberg, (arrow) 8, Dawid Lech, middle 15, Dzha33, (helmet) 7, Everett Historical, 14, Getmilitaryphotos, (soldier) 7, top 21 , bottom 21 (soldier) 28, (man) 29, GUDKOV ANDREY, (whale) 29, Howard Barnes, 16, Iakov Filimonov, (elk) 8, Joop Hoek, top 22, luca85, (shell) Cover, Mark_Kostich, 10, mountainpix, bottom left 9, MyImages - Micha, top 15, NaturePhoto, 27, Neirfy, (dolphin) 18, Nosyrevy, (fish) 11, Number1411, (beetle) 13, Omelchenko, design element throughout, pets in frames, (turtle) 7, Samakai, top right 24, Shahnewaz Mahmood, bottom left 18, silver tiger, (droplets) 28, Sofiaworld, top left 24, Umlaut1968, (tank) 5, vvoe, bottom 22, Wendy Naepflin, (samurai) 13

Every effort has been made to contact copyright holders of material reproduced in this book. Any omissions will be rectified in subsequent printings if notice is given to the publisher.

All the internet addresses (URLs) given in this book were valid at the time of going to press. However, due to the dynamic nature of the internet, some addresses may have changed, or sites may have changed or ceased to exist since publication. While the author and publisher regret any inconvenience this may cause readers, no responsibility for any such changes can be accepted by either the author or the publisher.

Printed and bound in the United Kingdom.

Contents

Inspired by nature 4

Ancient defences 8

Defences in the modern age ...14

The future is now! 20

    Glossary 30

    Find out more 31

    Index 32

Words in **bold** are in the glossary.

Inspired by nature

More than 100 years ago, in 1915, a new machine rumbled onto the battlefield. It was large and slow. But it went where most vehicles could not. It was made from thick metal. It did not have wheels. Instead, it had **tracks** that gripped the ground. It was the first tank.

During World War I (1914–1918), wheeled vehicles often got stuck in the mud. But a tank's tracks act like a caterpillar's legs. The tracks help tanks to move through mud and over objects.

Tanks have come a long way since World War I. But the main design has stayed the same. And it's all thanks to the tiny caterpillar.

FACT

The Allied Powers defeated the Central Powers in World War I. The Central Powers included the countries of Germany, Austria-Hungary and Turkey. The Allied Powers included Great Britain, France, Italy, the United States and other countries.

- Allied Powers
- Central Powers
- Neutral countries

tank tracks

Copying nature

In the wild, animals must compete to survive. Some animals have sharp claws or teeth. Others have strong defences to protect themselves. Some animals, such as tortoises, have a hard shell. Some animals can fly; others are good at hiding.

Military scientists study animals closely to invent new weapons and equipment. It makes sense. Animals have developed their natural skills over millions of years. Scientists use what they learn to make new defences for soldiers. Copying nature this way is called **biomimicry**. Animals have sparked many ideas for better armour, **camouflage**, robots and more.

Copying from nature is nothing new. Armies have done this for thousands of years. Throughout history, nature has provided new ideas to protect soldiers in the armed forces.

> **FACT**
> The word "biomimicry" comes from two Greek words. *Bios* means "life" and *mimesis* means "to imitate" (copy).

Helmets are hard like a tortoise shell.

camouflage uniform

7

Ancient defences

The first armour

Long ago, people used bows and arrows or clubs. Some used stone axes. These weapons were simple, but they were still deadly. People needed protection.

arrow with stone tip

Animal skins provided leather to make armour and shields.

Humans made the first defences directly from animals. They **tanned** animal skins. This process turns animal skins into leather. They used hardened leather to make simple body armour and shields. It helped to protect fighters from simple weapons.

Leather armour and shields worked well for a long time. But leather was later replaced by a stronger material – metal.

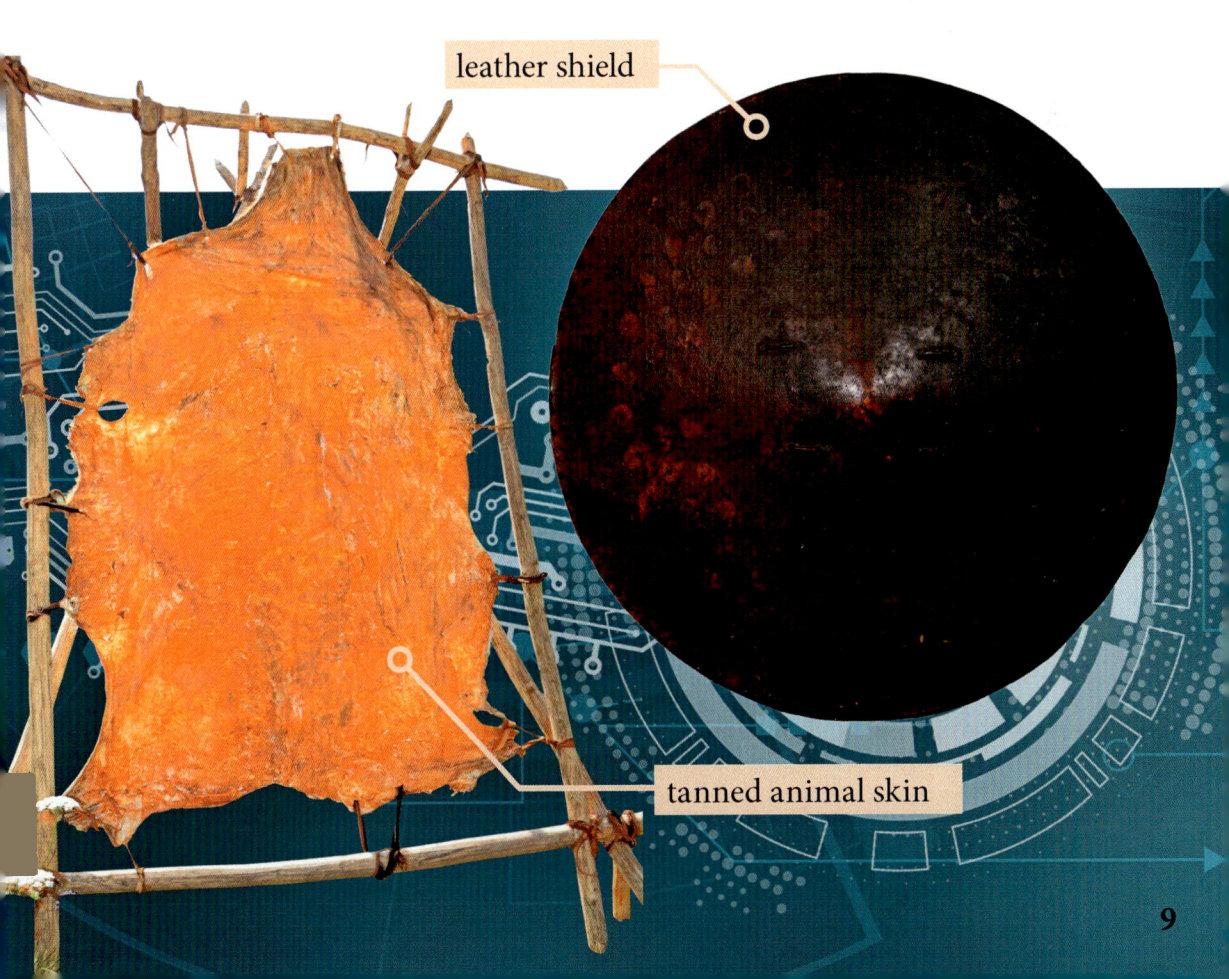

leather shield

tanned animal skin

The age of metal

Thousands of years ago, people began making metal tools from bronze and iron. They also made strong metal axes, swords and spears. Defences had to become stronger.

The first metal armour was called scale armour. It imitated reptile scales. It was made with small, overlapping metal plates. It worked well against blows from heavy weapons.

Soldiers later wore chain mail armour. It was made of small iron rings linked together. This armour acted like fish scales. It was lightweight and flexible. Soldiers could move and fight more easily in chain mail.

Knights in Europe wore full suits of armour. The metal suits acted like an insect's **exoskeleton**. This hard outer layer of an insect's body protects it from enemies. Armoured suits protected knights during battle.

Scale armour acted like a snake's scales.

FACT

Roman soldiers used the tortoise formation. They gathered together and overlapped their metal shields. This move formed a shell-like structure to protect the soldiers.

Chain mail was like fish scales.

Solid armour acted like an insect's hard outer shell.

Fear as defence

Metal armour was useful in battle. But sometimes making enemies fear you could work just as well. Armed forces copied nature to do this too.

The samurai were Japanese warriors. Some wore helmets with large horns like a deer. Other helmets looked like horned beetles. Enemy soldiers often ran from the warriors wearing these frightening helmets.

In Central America the Aztec people respected strong animals. Jaguar Knights and Eagle Warriors were fierce fighters. They wore armour covered with feathers, furs and claws. They also wore frightening helmets that looked like these mighty beasts.

The end of heavy armour
Gunpowder was invented more than 1,000 years ago. Armies soon learned to use it in cannons, bombs and guns. Heavy armour suits didn't work well against these powerful weapons. About 200 years ago, troops stopped wearing much armour. They wanted to move faster in battle. Soldiers mainly just wore metal helmets to protect their heads.

Some samurai helmets had horns like a rhinoceros beetle.

Aztec Eagle Warrior

13

Defences in the modern age

Looking to the sky

By 1900 battlefields became even more deadly. To protect troops, military defences had to change once again. The newest defences would soon be found in the sky.

Humans had long dreamed about flying. Then Orville and Wilbur Wright invented the first successful aeroplane in 1903. They shaped the plane's wings like a bird's wings. The shape allowed the plane to lift off the ground. Aeroplanes would soon change battlefields forever.

Wright brothers' *Flyer II* in 1904

A biplane's wings imitate the shape of bird wings.

Flying above enemies gives armies a big advantage in battle. Early in World War I, aeroplanes were used only for defence. Pilots flew high to find enemies. They sent information back to their ground troops. Leaders could then form a useful battle plan.

Hiding in plain sight

The ocean was another dangerous battlefield in World War I. German U-boats destroyed many British ships. These **submarines** often attacked without warning.

The British Navy found an amazing solution. They studied how zebra stripes confuse **predators** such as lions. This gives zebras extra time to escape.

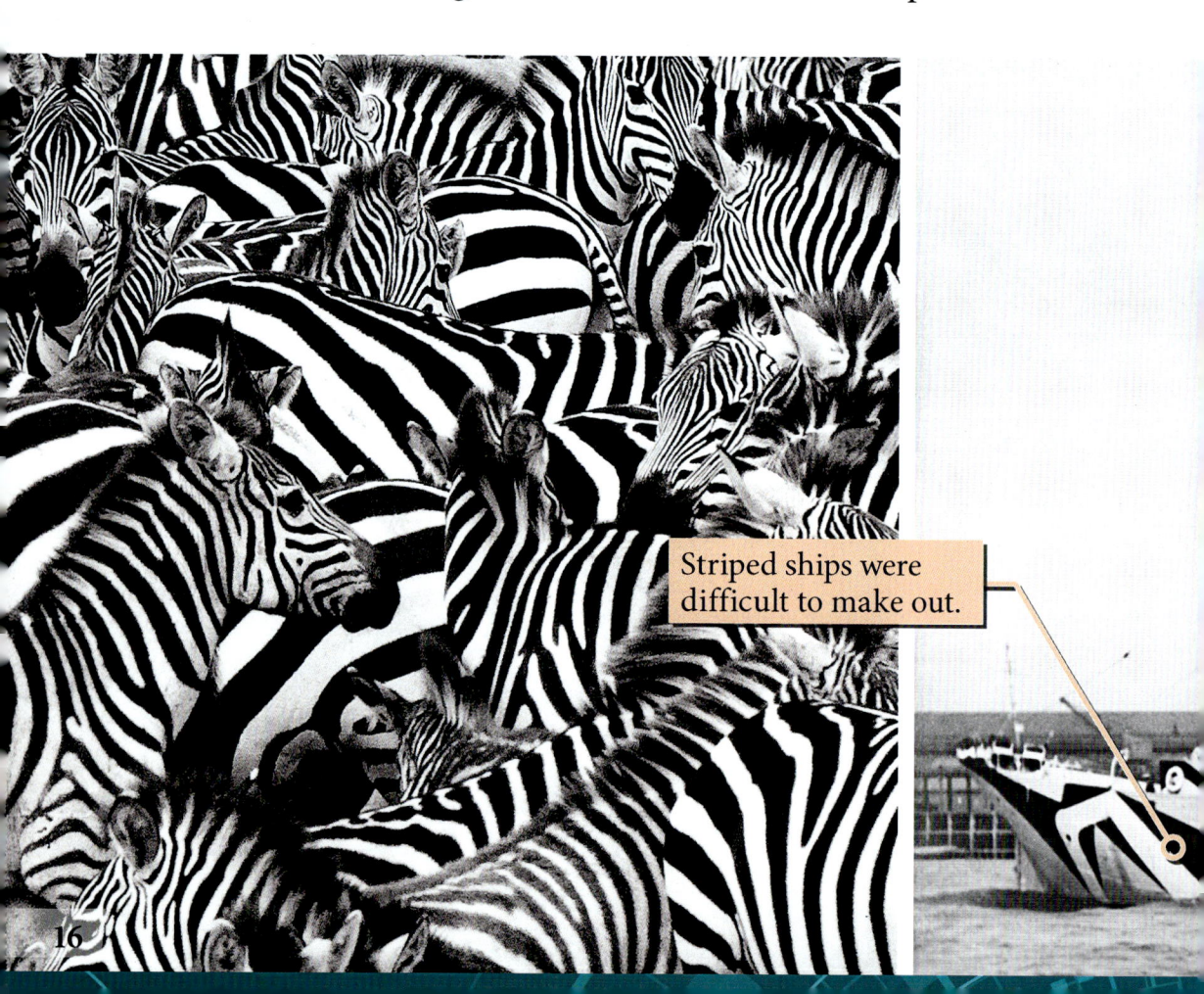

Striped ships were difficult to make out.

The navy followed nature's example. It began painting ships in black and white stripes. They called it dazzle camouflage. Almost 3,000 British ships were painted this way. The plan worked. The number of U-boat attacks soon dropped. The bold patterns confused U-boat crews. This gave British ships time to get away.

Beneath the waves

Some animals have natural **sonar** called **echolocation**. Dolphins make squeak and click sounds. The sounds bounce off fish back to the dolphins. Hearing the sounds helps them to locate food in the ocean.

Sonar works in the same way. Sound waves are sent out that bounce off objects. The speed of the returning waves is then measured. This information helps us to find hidden rocks, bombs or other objects in the water.

Sonar works like a dolphin's echolocation.

FACT
The US Navy began training dolphins about 50 years ago. They carry cameras and use their sonar to find underwater bombs.

Ships first used sonar more than 100 years ago. It helped to find hidden icebergs. Armed forces soon learned to use it too. During World War I, sonar helped find submarines.

The future is now!

Today's soldiers fight all over the world. And they don't just fight the enemy. They must often survive extreme heat, cold and dry conditions. Thanks to animals, their defences are becoming better than ever. Many new inventions are helping to protect troops on the battlefield.

Future machines

Many future defences are being made in the United States by the Defense Advanced Research Projects Agency (DARPA). Scientists at DARPA work on amazing new inventions based on nature. For example, the Soft Exosuit works like an insect's exoskeleton. It gives soldiers extra support to carry heavy loads.

An exosuit provides extra support like a beetle's exoskeleton.

soldier in cold-weather gear

soldier in warm-weather gear

Stronger, faster, lighter

Soldiers may soon have tough new armour. And it's thanks to some of nature's most unusual animals. Molluscs are simple creatures. But they have tough shells. Their shells protect them from pounding ocean waves and hungry predators.

molluscs

Scientists have long known about mollusc shells. But they have been difficult to copy. Now, thanks to **3-D printers**, scientists can copy the mollusc's special shell design. They hope to soon design new armour and helmets that are lighter and stronger.

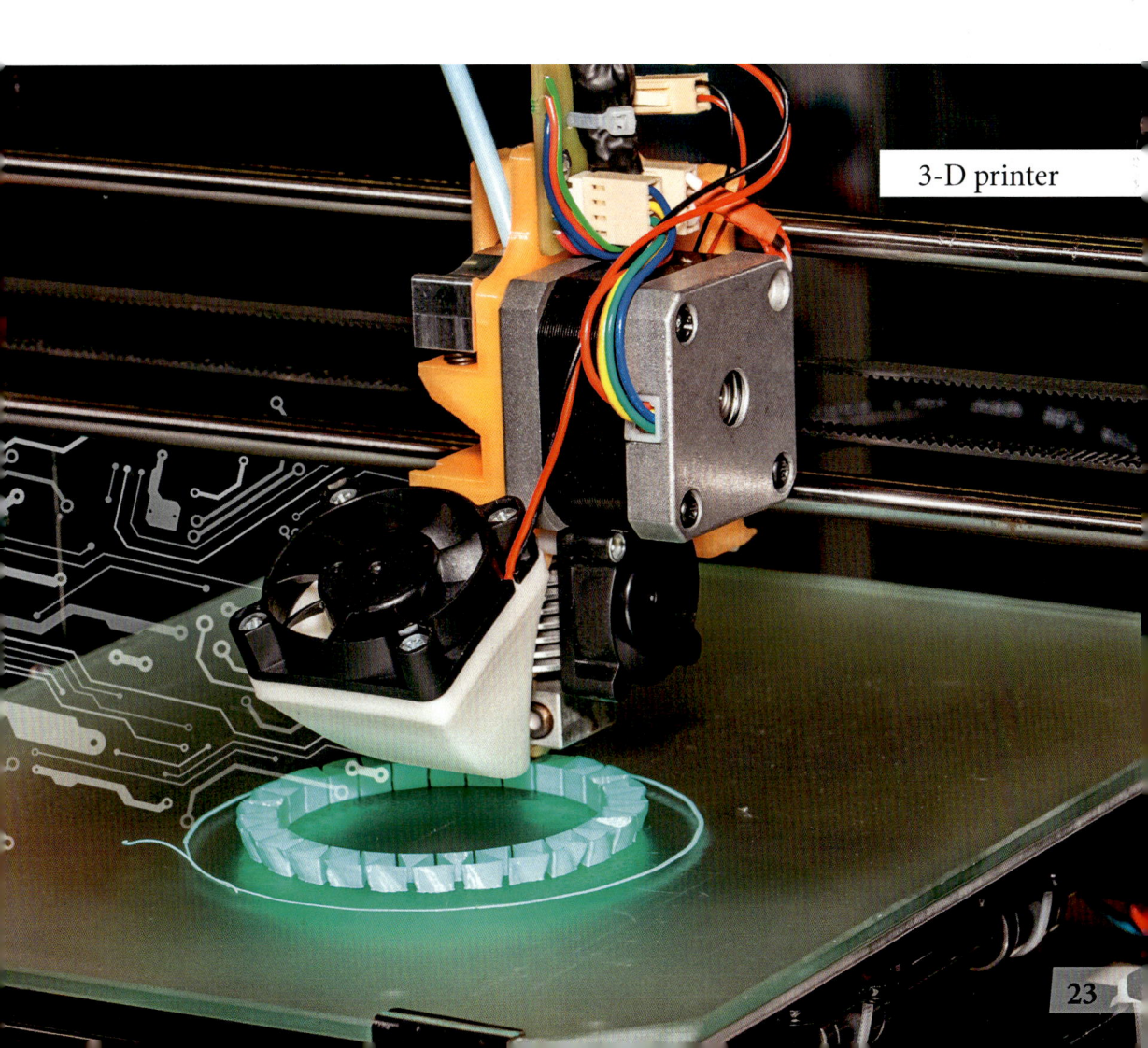

3-D printer

silk spider

silkworms

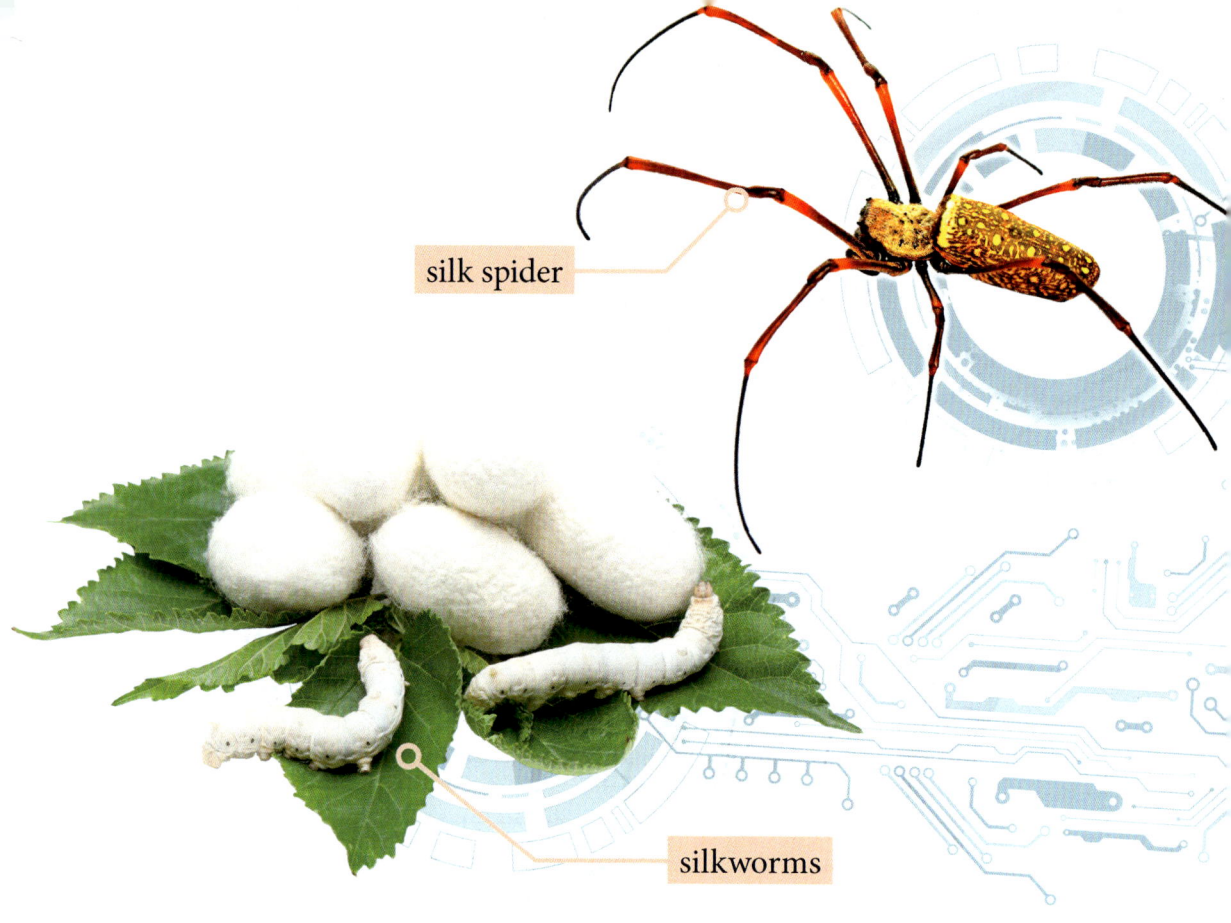

The strength of silk

Silk is made by spiders and silkworms. It is used to make cloth that is lightweight but strong. After World War I, pilots began using silk **parachutes**. If their planes were shot down, pilots needed a safe way to return to the ground.

Silk is playing a role in new defences too. The US Air Force is testing silk made from new materials. It is lightweight and even stronger than natural silk. Researchers hope to use the new silk to make armour that is lightweight and cool.

silk parachute

Next-level camouflage

Like many animals, soldiers often use camouflage to hide from enemies. Today scientists are working to design the camouflage of tomorrow. They're studying Earth's strangest creatures to do it.

> **FACT**
> Researchers are also working to hide a person's body heat. New uniforms may help troops to hide when enemies use heat-sensing equipment.

soldier in camouflage

Some ocean animals, such as squid and octopuses, can change colour in seconds. Sometimes they even make their skin appear rough or smooth, so they can blend in with the area around them.

The US military is working to copy this ability. Future uniforms may change colour instantly. They will help soldiers to hide on the battlefield.

octopus

Survive!

In Africa's Namib Desert, darkling beetles have special shells. They are covered in tiny bumps. The shell can collect moisture from the air. The water then drips into the beetle's mouth. Scientists are working to copy the beetle's shell. If successful, new water-collecting gear could help soldiers to survive in dry deserts.

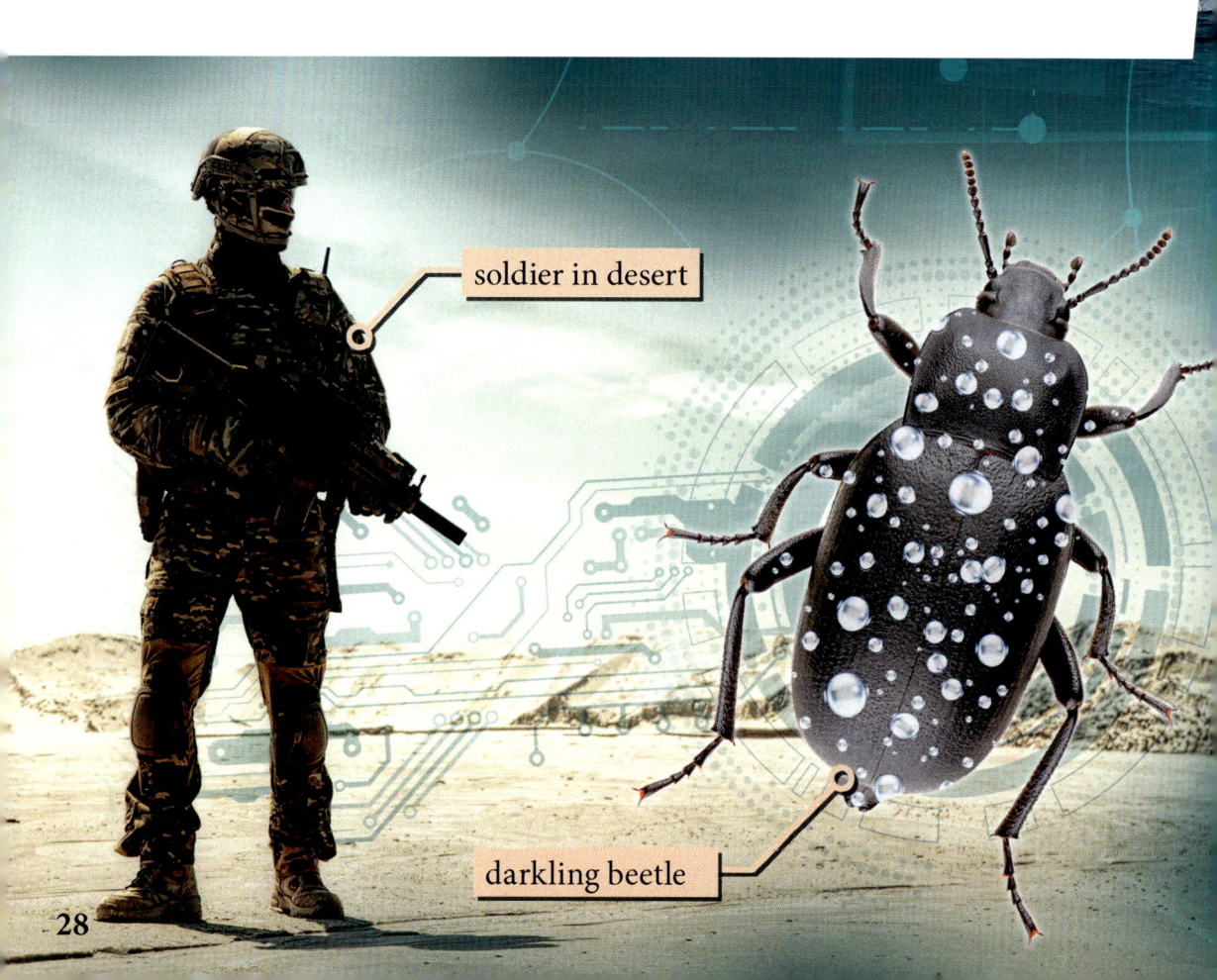

soldier in desert

darkling beetle

Future wetsuits may hold body heat like a whale's blubber.

Scientists are designing new wetsuits based on nature. Penguin feathers trap body heat. Whales and dolphins have a thick layer of blubber that traps heat. Future wetsuits may copy these animals. New materials can better trap body heat. The new wetsuits will help troops survive freezing waters.

Scientists are working hard to invent tomorrow's defences. Armed forces have copied nature's defences for a long time. Who knows what nature-based gear will be invented next?

Glossary

3-D printer device that uses a computer program to create objects

biomimicry copying the design of a living thing

camouflage patterns or colours that help animals or people to blend in with the area around them

echolocation process of using sounds and echoes to locate objects

exoskeleton hard outer shell of an insect

parachute large piece of cloth used to float slowly and safely to the ground

predator animal that hunts other animals for food

sonar device that uses sound waves to find underwater objects; sonar stands for sound navigation and ranging

submarine ship that can travel under the water

tan clean, treat and dry animal skins to turn them into leather

track links that form a loop on which some vehicles travel

Find out more

Books

Animals (DKfindout!), DK (DK Children, 2016)

Animals That Hide (Adapted to Survive), Angela Royston (Raintree, 2014)

Cars, Trains, Ships and Planes: A Visual Encyclopedia to Every Vehicle, DK (DK Children, 2015)

Secrets of World War I (Top Secret Files), Sean McCollum (Raintree, 2018)

Websites

www.bbc.co.uk/programmes/p011mr07
Learn more about camouflage in nature.

www.dkfindout.com/uk/history/world-war-i/tank-warfare
Find out more about tank warfare during World War I.

Index

3-D printers 23

animal defences 6
animals
    bats 18
    birds 14
    caterpillars 4
    darkling beetles 28
    deer 12
    dolphins 18, 19, 29
    fish 10
    horned beetles 12
    molluscs 22–23
    octopuses 27
    penguins 29
    reptiles 10
    silkworms 24
    spiders 24
    squid 27
    tortoises 6, 11
    whales 29
    zebras 16
animal skins 9
armour 9, 10, 12
Aztec warriors 12

biomimicry 6

camouflage 6, 26
    dazzle camouflage 17

Defense Advanced Research
    Projects Agency (DARPA) 20

echolocation 18
exoskeletons 10, 20

gunpowder 12

helmets 12

military defences 6, 9, 10, 11, 14,
    15, 20, 24, 29

Namib Desert 28

scientists 6, 20, 23, 26, 28, 29
shields 9, 11
special gear
    parachutes 24
    silk 24
    Soft Exosuit 20
    sonar 18–19
    uniforms 26, 27
    water collectors 28
    wetsuits 29

vehicles
    aeroplanes 14, 15
    submarines 16–17, 19
    tanks 4

World War I 4, 5, 15, 16, 19, 24
Wright, Orville and Wilbur 14